The Awkward Introvert's Party Survival Guide

David D.H. Shin

Table Of Contents

Chapter 1 : Introduction

Hello introverted reader, my name is David. I, like you, am an awkward introvert who dreads leaving the house and socializing with others. I've spent many hours at parties, awkwardly fiddling with my phone, because I'm not sure how to interact with other human beings. I worry that I'll say something inappropriate and unacceptable to someone, and as a result, my life will somehow be ruined. I don't have many interesting things to say, and assume that people don't want to hear from me anyways. Sometimes, even the prospect of socializing is anxiety inducing and completely drains all of my energy. If you can relate to what I just described, this book is for you.

So the title of this book might confused some of you. You might find yourself wondering, "Why do introverts need to survive parties at all? Can't they just stay home?" There are two things wrong with this assumption.

First, even the most introverted person needs social interaction. Socializing is not something we enjoy doing, but it is vital to our survival and to maintaining good mental health. It's like when you kill a cockroach, and you need to check to make sure it's crushed body is under the book you used to kill it.

You don't want to look at it because it's gross, but if you don't, you'll drive yourself crazy worrying that it's somewhere in your room plotting its revenge.

Second, introverts can find themselves in situations that require them to attend parties despite their desire to stay home. For example, if a person invites a good-hearted, introverted friend to a bachelor or bachelorette party, the introverted friend will attend. Sure, the introverted friend might rather rub their face with a cheese grater than attend a days long party, but even introverts understand that attendance at certain events is necessary. We introverts are awesome like that.

Now, I must stress that I am not some sort of psychologist or even someone who took an online course on the subject and printed a certificate of completion. I'm probably not super qualified to advise people on this topic, but I definitely have a lot of experience surviving parties as an awkward introvert. So I'm probably just regularly qualified. Regular is sometimes better than super, though, like a regular volcano eruption is much better than a supervolcano eruption. Anyhow, over the years of surviving many social gatherings, I've picked up tips and tricks on making the socialization a little more bearable.

I have been an introvert for as long as I can remember. My dream was to go to art school and become a lonely artist. A tortured soul who isolates himself to dig up the rawest form of human emotion to paint onto a canvas. Somewhere along the way though, through a series of unfortunate events, I became a consultant. As in, someone who interacts with clients, every day, to consult them about stuff. My lifelong dream of avoiding people fell hilariously unfulfilled, and instead, I got a job where I'm talking to people on an everyday basis. Because of these turn of events, I needed to learn how to adjust. I feel, because I do this everyday, that it gives me some level of credibility.

Even if you are an extrovert, I still recommend giving this book a read. You won't be able to relate to any of it, but you might gain a new perspective and appreciation for your introverted friends. Things that come naturally to you might take an introvert hours of preparation and heaps of effort. The next time you invite an introvert to your party and they accept, you'll understand the true cost of their acceptance. This is the same reason I read books about quantum physics. I don't understand any of it, but I am comforted by the fact that someone out there understands it and uses it to make the world a better place.

Now take a deep breath. Remember this moment. Mark the date on the calendar because your life will never be the same. Welcome, to the Awkward Introvert's Party Survival Guide! (I love it when they mention the title within the show!)

Chapter 2 : Developing Your Arrival Plan

The first step in participating in a party, is to arrive at the party. This seems straightforward, obvious, and not worth mentioning, but the fact that I am mentioning it should tell you that you are wrong. There are things you need to consider, even for the arrival to a party, to make sure you don't put yourself in awkward situations. Hours before the stated start time of the party, you need to develop a solid "arrival plan". I used to be a naive fool with no arrival plan once upon a time. I, probably like you, didn't think that an arrival plan was necessary. I was painfully wrong. Why do you think NASA does so much prep before blasting off into space? It's because they are carefully crafting their arrival plan in case they have to attend an alien space party (just trust me and don't fact check me on that).

The Around Buffer and Punctuality Index

When I was in college, I was invited to a get-together at a newly acquainted friend's apartment. I was told that people would start arriving at around 7:00 PM. I didn't know a lot of the people that would be coming, so I made sure to arrive punctually at

7:00 PM to make a good impression. Now, can you point out all the mistakes young David made?

First, I heard "get-together" and immediately lowered my guard because it didn't sound as bad or socially heavy as a party. Never make the mistake of thinking that a get-together is somehow more laid back and less social than an actual party. They are the same thing. Trust me, there are no rules or regulations on what can legally be called a get-together or a party. This is a common extrovert's trick to disarm introverts and get them to agree to coming to their party. You must never lose focus and be alert at all times when it comes to socializing. This is not a game folks.

Second, I didn't build in any buffer time, even though I was told that people would start arriving at "around" 7:00 PM. There is a big difference between something starting at 7:00 PM and starting at around 7:00 PM. You need to remember to add in at least 10 minutes buffer time when the party organizer uses the word "around." This extra added time is call the Around Buffer.

Third, I didn't do any background research on the people that would be attending the get-together. This is important and necessary to calculate the Punctuality Index. What is a Punctuality Index, you ask? The Punctuality Index of a party or gathering is the amount of time it takes from the stated start time, until the party actually gets started. For example, the Punctuality Index of a business meeting is usually much shorter than the Punctuality Index of a hang out at your best friend's house. You can't keep your boss waiting, but who cares if your friend Bobby has to wait an extra hour for you to show up. If this were a get-together with people I knew, I would already know the Punctuality Index, but I had no idea with this group of people. I could have discreetly asked the host about the group's punctuality or stalked everyone on Facebook to see if they were tagged in any "Tag the person who is always late" memes, but I didn't. The Punctuality Index has the potential to increase or decrease the Around Buffer.

Due to my lack of arrival plan, I took the 7:00 PM start time at face value and arrived at 7:00 PM. The terrible consequence of my failure to plan? I ended up being the very first person to arrive and spent 15 minutes ALONE with the host of the get-together. I shudder at the memory of those horrific 15 minutes. It was a full quarter hour of awkwardly sitting on the sofa with the host, pretending like my phone vibrated with a notification when it didn't, and desperately trying to think of something interesting to say. After talking about our days (which took a full 3 minutes), we struggled to keep the small talk going. We didn't know each other well enough to ask anything beyond those generic questions. Both of us literally jumped up and almost applauded when the next person arrived at the end of the 15 minutes of torture.

Now do you see why the Around Buffer and Punctuality Index is so important? Properly developing your arrival plan with the consideration of these two important factors will ensure that there will already be at least a few people at the party before you arrive.

Party Occasion

Parties usually have a reason for existing. A purpose for its being, if you will. A few popular reasons for having parties are birthdays, graduations, or even engagements. Parties are often celebrations to commemorate an accomplishment or anniversary of some sort. Of course, though, there are parties that have no purpose beyond socializing as well.

If you are sure that the party you are attending is of the latter type, then you are golden. No need to worry. If you aren't sure though, you need to make sure. Figure out what the occasion is and be certain you attend with the socially acceptable attire or objects.

For example, if it is a birthday party you are attending, you need to bring a present, or at the very least, a birthday card. This is to avoid the potentially awkward situation of entering the party and being directed toward the gift table, but not having anything to deposit there. If it is a graduation party, you need to at least find out who is graduating and from which institute of education.

Think about how awkward it would be if you went to a party on Halloween and assumed it would be a costume party. You walk in, dressed as a vampire, and the whole party stares at you. To your horror (you know, since it's Halloween), you realize that it's not a costume party. It's actually a party to celebrate Joe overcoming his irrational fear of caped men from Transylvania. Because you didn't know the occasion of the party, you now look like a silly, blood-sucking jerk.

I'm not saying that you need to be 100% prepared for every possible party occasion, but at least be aware of why the party is happening. Even if you don't have enough time to pick up a present for someone's birthday, if you know whose birthday it is, you can at least apologize for not bringing a gift and explain yourself. The name of the game is to not get caught off guard as to the purpose of the gathering.

Parking

If the party is at a location with plenty of parking, this won't be an issue. The situation where you do need to include your parking strategy as a part of your arrival plan is when parking is FILO (first in, last out). There are some places where people must park behind each other that causes the first car to be the last one to be able to get out. This is the FILO Factor. You must NEVER allow your car to be first in. Do you know how awkward it is to ask an entire party to move their cars so you can leave? We both know you'll never be able muster the courage to do this. You'll end up stuck at the party until everyone who parked behind you leaves.

You don't need to be the last person to the party because asking one or two people to move their cars is not that bad, but you most definitely do not want to be the first one in. If you have a clear understanding of the party's Punctuality Index, you should be able to ensure that your car is parked in front of three cars max. Make sure you bake in the FILO Factor into your arrival plan.

Relationship Status

People in relationships usually bring their significant others to the parties they attend. If one person in a relationship shows up at a party without their partner, it's natural to ask where they are. The typical answer is, "He/she is with his/her family" or, "He/she is at school/work." The moment this can turn disastrous, is if they have to answer, "We actually broke up/got divorced." How would you respond to that? Are you going to ask more personal questions to see why they are no longer together? Of course not. The only option at this point is to awkwardly apologize, walk away, and spend the remainder of the party in a hidden corner writhing in painful awkwardness.

You must remember to do research before the party to make sure people are still together. This isn't always straightforward, because while most people simply change their relationship status, there are people who don't change their relationship status until months after the actual split. You need to read between the lines. Has the person been only uploading pictures of themselves without their partner recently? Have they gone radio silent on social media? These might be signs that they are no longer together.

Unless you are absolutely sure that they are together, because they posted a photo together right before the party or something of the sort, then play it safe and assume they aren't together. It's better to be safe than sorry.

Political/Religious Views

Obviously, political and religious views are some of the most sensitive topics to discuss. If you are unaware of the most popular and accepted political or religious views of the group, it is best not to explore the subject. It is especially dangerous to assume that the mainstream, pop culture political and religious views will be the accepted views of the party.

Full disclosure, I am a Christian. At parties, I will make my religious convictions known through my actions and behavior, but I don't jump on a soapbox to preach. If anyone asks me about my faith, I don't shy away from having the discussion, but I don't do this uninvited. I've had situations where I am talking one-on-one with someone because they asked me about Christianity, but was overheard by someone with strongly negative views of my faith and decided to chime in. It was an unbelievably awkward and uncomfortable situation as I tried to address all of the issues he had with Christianity, but I did my best to be courteous and walk away from the topic to avoid creating resentment.

All this to say, imagine that the topic of politics and religion have one of those "Danger, Explosive

Content!" warning signs on it. I don't think it's bad to voice your opinion, if it is requested, but you need to be able to peacefully agree to disagree when opinions are not shared.

If you are at a party and you know that everyone shares the same political views and beliefs with you, then feel free to talk about it. If everyone has different views, but you are sure that the group can have a friendly, civilized discussion, then that is okay too. The situation you are trying to avoid is potentially offending someone by being too aggressive about your views.

Chapter 3 : Mastering Small Talk

Once you are at the party, the first thing you need to engage in is small talk. Small talk is the same thing as talking, but smaller. Okay, to be honest, I'm not sure what makes small talk different or special, but I just try to go with the flow. One thing I do know about small talk, though, is that small talk for extroverts is like the appetizer before a conversational meal.

It can be difficult to participate in small talk if you don't have any predetermined small talk topics, so the following are a few example small talk questions and topics that you can start your small talk with. Most of these will work for most party settings, but you need to feel out the party to see what is appropriate or not.

Small Talk Topics

1. How was your day?
    *   The response to this questions is, "Good, how about yours?" 99% of the time. Don't feel bad about replying back, "Good." Most people expect that.

- You don't need to feel pressured to actually talk about your day just yet. If you have something to say regarding your day, though, then of course feel free to talk about it. You just don't need to feel the anxiety of trying to figure out something interesting to say.
- Definitely make sure you don't respond back, "good, how about yours?" as well and get trapped in an endless loop.

2. How is your family?
- Do NOT ask this question if you know the person is an orphan.
- Don't forget the relationship status research in your arrival plan. You don't want to ask someone about their significant other if they are no longer together. The entire party turns quiet and, if you are unlucky, you might be responsible for making the person cry. As interesting it is to watch this in a movie, the awkwardness of being responsible is off the charts.

3. Anything interesting happen at work/school?
- Unless they are depressingly unemployed or have dropped out. Make sure you know for a fact that they are working or in school.
- This is what I meant when I said you need to, "feel out the party to see what

is appropriate." Asking questions that are inappropriate for the situation or person will land you smack dab in the middle of awkward island, in the middle of awkward ocean, stranded in the awkward forest.

4. Traffic, am I right?
    o   I live in Atlanta so this one is very popular. In Atlanta, everyone will have had to sit through traffic to get to the party, regardless of the day or time. Use your discretion on this one though. You don't want to ask someone about traffic if the party is at a college dormitory and no one drove to the party. They will quickly see through your pre-planned small talk topics and judge you.

5. How about the *insert local sports team*?
    o   Even if you are not a sports enthusiast, this is usually a safe small talk topic. If the person you are talking to is a sports enthusiast, you can ask this question and zone out for the next 5 minutes or so.
    o   If the person is not a sports enthusiast, they'll return a generic response like, "Yeah, how about them huh?" No one likes to admit they don't know much about sports. I've gotten away with using this one for years without really being interested in

sports. I'll memorize some quick facts about Lebron or Messi and make it seem like I know sports well. I do not.

6. Did you hear about the *insert relevant celebrity*?
   - Try Kim Kardashian and Kanye West. They're usually up to something crazy.
7. I saw this weird thing on the internet, have you heard about it?
   - The weird thing can be whatever is trending on Twitter or any social media platform really. One good example of this is the picture of the dress that some thought was blue with black stripes while others saw white with gold stripes.
   - The latest one, during the time of writing this, is the debate over whether you hear Yanny or Laurel.
8. I saw an interesting movie on Netflix the other day.
   - This one isn't a question. It's a conversation starting statement. Most people will ask you what the movie's title was and what the plot is. As long as you have a genuine reason for believing the movie was interesting, this is an easy conversation starter. You don't need to be funny or clever during this conversation. All you're doing is recounting a movie you liked.

9. Did you know that *insert interesting fact here*

- Look up some of those "interesting facts" websites and memorize a few that truly surprised you. Like, did you know that some fungi create zombies, then control their minds? I just googled that real quick. You can jump off that and talk about how a zombie apocalypse isn't too far fetched and start constructing a zombie apocalypse survival plan.
- Don't spend the entire party reciting your interesting facts, though. You don't want to become the weird guy at parties that spouts off irrelevant facts.

10. What do you enjoy doing in your spare time?

- A good question to ask people you don't know well. You can learn a lot about people from what their hobbies are.
- For example, if someone responds, "I usually rope it to a tree branch and swing on it" and they clarify your confusion by saying, "Oh, spare time? I thought you said spare tire!" and laugh like a maniac, then they are probably a dad who loves lame dad jokes.

Small Talk Exit Strategy

Now that you have successfully engaged in small talk, you need to have an exit strategy handy. Usually, the small talk comes to a natural and comfortable end and both parties can part ways to do something else, but there are two situations where an exit strategy will be essential: the small talk ends too early or drags on too long.

Imagine this. You are at a party and you run into an acquaintance. He or she asks you how your day was. You respond, "Good" and reciprocate the question. He or she also responds, "Good." Silence. Neither of you know what to do because the duration of the small talk clearly wasn't long enough to declare it successful. You take a sip of your drink to buy some time, but you can't formulate a plan. Awkwardness continues until your small talk companion simply decides to walk away. You spend the rest of the party trying to avoid running into this person again. If you had a proper exit strategy, this could have easily been avoid.

There are two types of exit strategies you need to prepare before a party: the Closer and the Stop Loss.

The Closer can be used in the example situation I just presented. You've engaged in small talk that is cut far too short due to both person's inability to carry out a conversation. My favorite Closer is to pretend your phone just vibrated and that you've received an important text message or email. You can then simply say, "Sorry, I need to go make a phone call" and step outside for a few minutes. Just make sure you have a backstory ready incase people ask you if everything is okay. You can use a variation of that Closer or develop one of your own.

Remember, the goal is to fake an urgent reason for you to step outside, but nothing life changing like the death of a family member. You don't want to have to live the rest of your life making sure you don't post new photos of your sibling and posting annual, "I miss you, brother…" messages on social media.

The Stop Loss is for situations where small talk drags on for far too long. Never forget that extroverts are energized when socially engaged. Why do you, the introvert, think you get so tired? It's because the extrovert is draining that energy from you. For this reason, there can be many instances where an extrovert will bait an introvert into small talk and suck the life force out of him or her for hours. This is when having a Stop Loss exit strategy will come in handy. My favorite Stop Loss tactic is to pretend your phone just vibrated and that you've received an important text message or email. You can then simply put up a finger and say "Sorry, I need to go make a phone call" and leave the conversation mid-sentence. Make sure to put on your concerned face to avoid coming off as rude. Make up a "I thought my dog died, but it was a false alarm" story incase people ask what happened.

To the average person, the Closer and Stop Loss exit strategies may look identical and having two different names for them may seem superfluous. They are. Congratulations for noticing.

Why Small Talk?

Most of you reading this right now might be thinking, "Why don't I just get to the party really late so I can join when all the small talks over?" My dear introverted friend, that is a classic rookie mistake. You need to think of small talk as a sort of investment. You invest a little bit of your social energy up front so that you won't need to make a bigger deposit later.

After my disastrous experience of being the first party attendee for 15 minutes, I decided to go to my next party at least 30 minutes late. It seemed like a good idea at the time, but it totally backfired on me like a backwards pointed bazooka. What happened was that all of the small talk was over by the time I got there, so EVERYONE turned their attention toward me to ask me about my day and how I was doing. I stood in front of a semi-circle of people just lobbing questions at me one by one. As you could imagine, this was the worst night of my life.

Extroverts have a catch-up quota with every person they don't see on a regular basis. They go to parties and have small talk with each person until that quota is met. They can move on to other things once their small talk quota is met with every person at the party, but when you arrive late, they just see another quota that needs to be filled. That means every single extrovert at the party will sniff you out like a shark with blood in the water if you arrive late, and they haven't met their small talk quota with you. Dealing with extroverts one by one is not as bad as having a horde of extroverts attack you with small talk at once.

See? The small talk serves a purpose. It parses out social interaction into small, digestible chunks. I'm sure that you, as an introvert, are more than aware of the value of having a controlled stream of socialization and not an endless wave of it.

Chapter 4 : Names

Names. Everyone has got one. Actually, most people have two while some even have three. It's important to know names to effectively distinguish between one person and another. It's exhausting to describe someone every time you need to identify them. Believe me, I've tried. "So the bald guy with acne takes out a bat and starts swinging at the girl who used to date the guy who always wears the poncho, but the old man McBeardy took out a shotgun and pointed it to the bald guy with acne and the girl who used to date the guy who always wears the poncho starts crying on the dude with the really douchey hair's shoulder!" See? It's exhausting.

Names aren't as important in an one-on-one conversation. You rarely have to mention the name of the person you are talking to, but in a party setting, it is difficult to get away with calling everyone buddy, friend, guy, or sport.

The reason I mention names in this book is because they have huge amounts of AIP or "Awkwardness Inducing Potential." Because names are so closely tied to one's identity, an offense to the name can, subconsciously, be interpreted as an offense to the identity. Think about how hurt you were when your parents called you by a sibling's name, or that one time your boyfriend or girlfriend accidentally called you by their ex's name.

There are several situations where the misuse of names can place you in an inescapable pit of awkwardness. I've seen several introverts move out of town because of some of these situations. Those situations, and what to do during them, are as follows:

The "Who are you"

The "Who are you" is the awkward situation where you forget someone's name whom you've already met. There is nothing worse than being at a party with someone you barely know. Both of you know that you've already met, so it's not polite to not acknowledge them. The nightmare scenario, though, is when you can't quite remember what that person's name was, but you do know that you were introduced at one point. You obviously can't simply ask, "Sorry, what was your name again?" like a savage extrovert. Luckily, there are a few clever ways you can figure out the person's name without ever revealing that you forgot the person's name.

First method you can employ is the Faux Introduction. You grab a friend that you know and ask the person whose name you have forgotten if he or she has met your friend. Nine out of ten times the conversation will go like this:

"Hey, have you met Nick?"
"Oh, not yet. Hi, my name is Barney."

If the two have already met, then your friend might just respond, "Yeah, I met Barney at the party last weekend." People tend to take the question, "Have you met so and so?" as a challenge and feel the need to prove themselves by reciting the person's name.

It's best to have a few "planted friends" at the party who know that you'll use them to figure out people's names. This way you'll have a fool-proof strategy to get yourself out of a "Who are you."

Another method you can employ is the Odd Spelling. This one is a bit trickier than the Faux Introduction, but it does not require a planted friend to pull off. Let's face it, most of us are too awkward to even ask a friend to be a plant for the Faux Introduction.

The Odd Spelling can be used during the middle of a conversation by simply asking, "So I may be mistaken, but are you the one who spells their name weird? How do you spell your name again?" Not knowing the spelling of the person's name is acceptable since people are usually verbally introduced. If you were introduced through an app or text message, though, then pull out your phone and look at it. You dummy.

Anyhow, whatever the response to your question may be, simply come up with an odd spelling for it and say, "Oh, nevermind. I thought you were the one who spelt it 'Kris' with a K." Here are a few common names and different spellings that you may be able to use.

Ordinary Name	Odd/Uncommon Spelling
Brian	Bryan
Kelly	Kelley
Andrew	Andru
Daniel	Daneel
Jack	Jaque
Shirley	Surely
Elizabeth	Elisabeth
Michael	Mikael
Joseph	Josef
Victor	Viktor
Jim	Gym

It doesn't matter that a lot of these spellings aren't really used. If they ask, "Who spells Shirley as 'Surely'?" you just respond, "I know right? It was different and I forgot if it was you who spelt it that way."

The "Not quite you"

The "Not quite you" is when you mispronounce/misremember someone's name whom you've already met. This is only a slight variation of the "Who are you" but can be more offensive than if you had just forgotten their name all together.

There are two way this could play out. Either you know that you don't know how to pronounce their name or you don't know that you don't know how to pronounce their name.

The first situation is pretty easy. This usually is an issue with people whose names are of a different language or culture. In this scenario, it is perfectly acceptable to admit that you have forgotten how to pronounce it and ask them about it. Make it clear that you don't know how to pronounce it and make a polite attempt so they know that you haven't completely forgotten their name. You can approach it as follows:

"Hey, I'm so sorry but I don't think I know how to correctly pronounce your name. Is it David Sheen?"

"It's Shin like the part of your leg. Thanks for asking!"

See? Admitting that you don't know how to pronounce their name, in this instance, doesn't make the situation awkward. The other person will appreciate your cultural sensitivity and attempt to being respectful.

The second situation can be a bit trickier. If you go ahead and confidently blurt out their name and it turns out you mispronounced it, the only recourse is damage control. Have a few excuses ready that all point to you being stupid. You don't want to say something like, "Oh sorry, your name is so hard to pronounce." That will make the other person feel like their name and identity are being attacked or mocked. You need to say something more along the lines of, "Oh sorry! I am always terrible at names!" or, "My tongue is so stiff and I never learned to roll my R's" or even, "I got dropped as a baby so the part of the brain that correctly pronounces things got damaged."

Once the situation is diffused, you can move on with your conversations. Make sure to verbally say their name out loud, at least two or three times, throughout the duration of the party. Not only will it help you remember their name for next time, it should go a long way in repairing the damage to their ego that you caused.

The "That's not you"

The "That's not you" is where you mistake a stranger for someone you've already met. You extend out your hand for a handshake and say, "Hey Fred!" only to see confusion dawn on the other person's face as he responds, "Uh... I'm Joseph." I've never had this happen to me personally, but I don't know if I would survive such an awkward situation. If you think that mistaking someone's name will bruise their ego, try mistaking their entire identity. Like the second situation in "Not quite you", all you can do is damage control.

The only thing you can do in this situation is apologize profusely and discretely compliment that person. You can say things like, "I can't believe I mistook you for Fred! You are much better looking than he is!" This may seem distasteful because you end up slightly insulting the person you thought was your partymate, and it is. What are you going to do though, right? You need to break a few eggs to make an omelet. You've got to rip open the bandage wrapping to apply the bandage and heal the wound.

That is all I'm going to say about this situation because it's making me feel uncomfortable just thinking about it.

The "Who am I"

The "Who am I" is when someone you've already met obviously forgot your name, but is too awkward to ask.

This is a very simply situation to remedy. If someone keeps referring to you or calling you without using your name, it's safe to assume that they've forgotten it. Don't worry, I know what you're thinking. You won't need to awkwardly say anything like, "Um… my name is David by the way." There are sneakier ways to announce your name. For example, you can slyly sneak your name into a story.

My favorite story to tell in this situation is a story I call "the name tag incident." The story goes:

"So I went to a conference for work a few years back in Las Vegas. I went to sign-in at the registration table, but I couldn't find my name tag where all the name tags were laid out. I started to freak out because I couldn't remember if I properly registered or not. This was an important conference that I needed to attend and there were no more spots left. Then finally, I realized that the reason I couldn't find my name tag is because it was in the S's under Shin, David. I was looking at the D's the whole time!"

A quick and easy to remember story about name tags that enables the hearers to be reminded of your name. Of course, with everything else in this book, you can feel free to tell the story exactly like mine or develop your own.

The last resort can be to just buy name tags and wear one to every party you attend. You can be that weird name tag guy. I don't recommend it, but it certainly is an option I suppose.

The "That's not me"

The "That's not me" is when someone mistakes you for someone else they've already met. If this happens, just correct the person, but assure him or her that it is a common mistake that many people make. The goal here is to suppress your own awkwardness and act like it's not a big deal. Even if no one has ever mistaken you for this person in question, and you have no idea who this person is, just say something like, "It's no problem at all! We get mistaken for each other all the time like Katy Perry and Zooey Deschanel." If you are able to diminish the severity of the mistake, the ensuing awkwardness will be minimized.

In high school, I was mistaken for other people all the time. I fashioned a hairstyle that was very popular to other Asian males, so from the back we all looked indistinguishable. One day, while I was sitting in the library playing chess, a stranger walked up behind me, put his arm across my shoulder and asked, "So how was the pre-calc test?" I had no idea what he was talking about because I was taking AP Calculus at the time. After the stranger sensed my confusion, he looked at me and said, "Oh my bad! I thought you were my friend!" and walked away.

I spent the remainder of my time in highschool simply avoiding this stranger, because it was too awkward for me. My awkwardness at the situation increased the amount of awkwardness for this stranger as well. If we saw each other in the hall, we would both turn around and walk the other way. I never learned this stranger's name, but he is responsible for the majority of the anxiety that I felt walking the halls of my high school.

If I had known any better, I would have powered through the awkwardness and played it cool. My non awkward response would have minimized the awkwardness that he felt as well. Because I failed to nip the situation in the bud, I suffered the consequences for years.

The "I Don't know you"

This last scenario will be the most familiar to the introverts reading this book. Remember the last time you went to a friend's party and didn't know most of the people there? You stood around without the courage to introduce yourself, so you stuck by your friend's side as if you two were siamese twins. Your friend knew most of the people at the party so you hoped with all your heart that your friend would organically introduce you to everyone else.

If you have the type of friends that do indeed make introductions for you, then you are blessed. Keep those friends forever and never take them for granted. They are the true MVPs of the world.

If your friends are the type to disappear into the crowd and leave you to fend for yourself, then you need to weed them out of your life. Right now.

I know that the right answer to this predicament is to be brave and introduce yourself. A simple, "I don't think we've met. My name is Blah Blah." It's one sentence. What's the worst that can happen right? I know it in my head, but my introverted heart cannot accept this. The amount of social energy required to introduce myself to strangers is beyond my capacity.

So in conclusion, if you feel bold enough to, the easiest solution is to introduce yourself. For the true introverts, though, just stick with friends that are sensible enough to introduce you to strangers, and stop talking to the ones that won't accommodate you in this way.

Other Thoughts

A few things before I wrap up on names. You'll notice that the "Not quite me", the scenario where someone mispronounces your name, is missing. This is not a mistake, I intentionally left it out. It's not the end of the world if someone pronounces your name wrong. I was at a party where someone called me Daveed the whole night because he, somehow, got the impression that I was from Mexico. It would have come off as pretentious for me to correct him like, "Um, actually, it's David." It's easier to just let this one go and hope someone else corrects him or her for you later when you're not around.

Lastly, there is some pre-party prep you can do to minimize running into any of the situations I have listed here. In the age of social media and Facebook, it shouldn't be too difficult to do some research of the party's attendees beforehand. Take some time to memorize their names and faces. Just make sure to not already know the name of someone you haven't met yet. Even if they are part of the same circle of friends as you, never admit that you've seen their profile pop up in your social media feed. It comes off as stalkerish if you already know someone you haven't met in person, even though everyone knows that everyone pops up in everyones feeds.

Chapter 5 : Finding the Conversational Entry Point

After a few minutes of small talk, it is normal for those individual conversations to merge into group conversations. It's easy to talk when the conversation involves only two people, but when the whole group is partaking in the conversation, it can be difficult to find the CEP or "Conversational Entry Point." The CEP is the small sliver of time after the last person to talk has finished speaking, but before so much time has passed that whatever you had to say is no longer relevant because a new topic was introduced.

I was recently part of a conversation about child rearing. As an Asian, at a mostly Asian gathering, it was basically just a conversation where everyone tried to one-up each other with stories about who got beat the worst as a child. As an introvert, I patiently listened as everyone took turns telling their story. With each story told, my anticipation grew. I knew I had the best story and I couldn't wait for my chance to tell it. Then, as the last person finished his story, I waited a few moments to make sure he was done. There was a moment that I said to myself, "This is it, I should tell my story now!" I didn't, though, and decided to give the previous storyteller a few more moments to add any last minute details. Unfortunately, some jerk changed the subject to the ethical dilemma of whether or not child rearing is actually helpful or actually damaging. I missed my timing and had to swallow my story. To this day, I have never had the opportunity to share the story of the epic beatdown I received as a child.

The moment I thought I should start talking was the CEP. The moment you allow your introverted nature to tell you to delay your story, is the moment you are too late. You need to go against your shy, introverted nature and be bold. Start talking and commit, even if it seems like someone else is going to say something. This is the only way your voice will be heard.

The following are two methods to ensure a successful entrance into the CEP:

The Clapper

The first CEP entry method is called the Clapper. It is just as it sounds. You clap. This works because it transitions well from clapping about the previous story, to your story. When you sense the end of someone's story, start clapping. You need to be a little bit obnoxious about the clapping, because it needs to be loud enough to confuse, maybe even startle, the people in the conversation. This brief moment of confusion will give you enough time to slip into the conversation with your story.

Make sure you only use this method during positively vibed scenarios. You don't want to use the

Clapper during a wake or funeral. Just read the room and be positive that clapping is appropriate.

The "Oh Oh Oh!"

In situations where clapping is inappropriate or impossible (maybe you're Captain Hook?), you can utilize the "Oh Oh Oh!" The trick to this method is to say "Oh Oh Oh!" like the previous person's story reminded you of a story of your own. Similar to the Clapper, your sudden outburst of noise will confuse and/or startle people long enough to allow comfortable entry into the CEP. It doesn't even have to be "Oh Oh Oh!" You can say anything that implies you've suddenly been reminded of something. Maybe say "Dude! Bro!" if you are at a frat party. I don't know, do whatever fits the situation.

The only risk in using the "Oh Oh Oh!" is that you'll need an actual, interesting story. This method, although great at startling the group, is too good at drawing attention. Actually, it goes beyond drawing attention, it incites excitement. After the initial shock and confusion wears off, people get excited about what they will assume is a good story. If you don't deliver, people may silently judge you.

Inevitability, though, when attempting entry into a conversation through the CEP, you may find yourself in a situation where you start to talk, but get cut off by someone else. Even when you go in strong and loud, there are always one or two self-centered jerks who only want their voices to be heard. Don't get discouraged by this. What you want to do in this situation is to simply concede. Let the douche-bag talk. You can punish him by withholding your awesome story from him forever.

Chapter 6 : Drinks?

If it is a non-alcoholic drink, then yes. It's always helpful to have something you can occupy your hands with. You don't want to find yourself pulling a Ricky Bobby and awkwardly holding your hands in the air because you don't know what to do with them. It's nice to have a beverage you can drink when you run out of things to say and need a few seconds to think of new topics. You can comment on how good or bad the drink is as well.

Alcoholic drinks may be tempting because they might help you loosen up, but my recommendation is to not drink any alcohol. Stay far away as possible. If you think making a fool of yourself in an awkward situation is bad, imagine the entire internet watching it the day after. I guarantee that people will film you acting like a drunk idiot and post it all over social media. They will be excited to do so, because they will not have seen that side of you before. To an extrovert, a video of a their drunk introverted friend is like finding a unicorn.

Attending a party is not game (I'm pretty sure I mentioned this at least once before). You need to stay alert and focused from the moment you leave your house until you get back. Alcohol will make you lose focus and all your preparation and research would have been for naught. For naught, I say!

Chapter 7 : Telling Interesting Stories

Okay. So, you've been at the party for long enough to be fairly comfortable. You've gone through the small talk, gotten introduced to everyone, and gained a good bearing of your surroundings. You're in the groove of the party and the awkwardness induced anxiety has died down.

If you read that and said, "What? I'm still terribly awkward and anxious being here," then sorry. I know that it's hard. There are going to be parties where you never really feel comfortable. Parties where you are steeped in anxiety for the entire duration. All you can do is soldier through them and hope the next one will be better.

If you agree with my first statement, though, then you might be ready for advance level socializing. Do you want to try telling some interesting stories and becoming the center of attention?

Woah there! Don't close the book just yet! I am not saying that telling stories is a necessity, but it can have some benefits. Just think of this chapter as a bonus chapter. If you absolutely don't want to interact with people beyond the bare necessity, then that's fine. Feel free to skip to the next chapter. If you feel extra bold and want to step out of your comfort zone a little, then read on. I am here to help you through it and make it not as awkward as possible.

The benefit of telling stories is that it shows people that you are an interesting person. We all know that you are funny, intelligent, and compassionate person that is wrapped up in a plethora of awkward and introverted layers. Those pesky layers of shyness prevent your true core from shining through. Now, we can't rip off all those layers in one sitting, but we can let a glimmer of your interesting core shine out bit by bit in the form of stories.

The fun part of being an awkward introvert that successfully tells an interesting story is, that no one will expect it and be pleasantly surprised. People get tired of hearing stories from the same people over and over again, but when an introvert graciously recites a funny and interesting story, the masses will rejoice and be moved to emotional tears of joy. Why? Because it's like watching a video of a deaf person hearing the voice of their loved ones for the first time.

The basic structure of a story is as follows:

1. The Set-Up
   - The set-up is the beginning of the story where you bring the audience into the setting and situation of the story. During this phase of the story, you should describe the setting and establish the relevant characters. Try to be a brief as possible. People have

increasingly shortened attention spans and it is possible to lose people's interest during this phase. Make sure you give all the necessary context and information though. Apply the Goldilock rule; not too short, but not too long either.

2. The Conflict
    o The conflict phase is when you describe the conflict. The conflict can be external (two people in disagreement) or internal (a person mentally debating whether or not to eat the last burger).
    o Does your story not have a conflict? Don't tell that story then. Stories without conflict are pointless and uninteresting.
    o Seriously, I love you as my amazing reader, but I'll disown you if you try to tell a story only describing a sandwich you ate for lunch. That's so pointless, man.

3. The Climax
    o The climax is the moment when the characters' conflict reaches its highest point. The part of the story that puts people on the edge or their seats. The sweat inducing moment that makes the audience ask, "So what happened next!?"

4. The Resolution

- The resolution is the answer to the question that the audience asks during the climax. How did the conflict get resolved?
- The ultimate resolution isn't necessary if it is a story of an ongoing conflict that you are experiencing.

Now that you understand the basic structure of storytelling, let me give you a few examples of stories. Let's see if you can identify the four phases in each of these stories.

The Acrobat

On my way to the party, I saw a man in a leotard swinging from tree to tree. I literally stopped and parked my car on the side of the road because it was such an odd sight. There weren't any cameras or crowds gathered, so it seemed like the guy was just doing this for fun. I sat there thinking about why he was doing this. I couldn't figure it out.

He swung to one side of the street, but made his way back to where I had parked my car. I waited for him to get closer and decided that I would ask him what he was doing. I'm an awkward introvert, so the prospect of talking to a stranger made me a bit anxious. I mustered up the courage, though, and shouted toward the man as he got closer.

"Excuse me! Can I ask why you are swinging from tree to tree?" I asked.

"Nope! Sorry!" the mysterious man replied.

43

So I just got back in my car and came to this party. I can't stop thinking about the leotard guy though. It's going to drive me crazy with curiosity.

Road Rage

I think there are unspoken rules of the road that we should all live by. Sure, there are laws dictating things you can and can't do on the road, but what I'm talking about are etiquettes of the road. For example, I hate it when someone rides the open lane of a highway to cut in front of a long line of people waiting for the exit lane.

I'm the type of person who considers it my civic duty to tail the cars in front of me as closely as possible, so that the people trying to cut in last minute won't be able to. I'll wait patiently on the exit lane, leaving just enough room to bait potential line cutters, and block them off at the last second so that they have to go back on the highway and miss their exit. I laugh as they honk at me and make vulgar gestures in their full on road rage. You don't need to thank me, I do it for the greater good.

So today, I was running late to work. Usually, even when I'm late, I keep my honor and wait on the exit lane. I'd rather be late than a line cutter. But I must've been distracted because they aired a story about the financial viability of a real life Batman. I was intrigued to say the least. I started daydreaming about becoming Batman myself and I came to a stark revelation: I was about to miss my exit.

As I drove by I noticed a huge opening for me to cut into. It was entirely possible that the car next to me was giving me an opening to cut in. I had an internal debate about the morality of the situation. Do I take this gift presented to me by a kind stranger or do I stick to my morals and choose not to cut in?

So after a few moments of careful consideration… I cut in. I know, I am a hypocrite, but I just couldn't pass it up.

The Weird Book

So I recently read this weird book that I found online. It's called "The Awkward Introvert's Party Survival Guide." It talks about all of the things awkward introverts need to think about and consider before attending a party. It also gives some suggestions on things you can do at parties to avoid awkward situations.

It talks about these obviously made up concepts like Punctuality Indexes and Conversational Entry Points. The book details these weirdly cool ways to get out of potentially awkward situations.

As an awkward introvert myself, it was a great read. It's funny and ridiculous at times, but it definitely captures the hardships that introverts go through in social settings. I could relate to so much of it, because I'm always sort of anxious about large group socializing like this.

It's a great book, though, you should definitely give it a read. Buy a few copies and pass it out to all your friends.

Chapter 8 : Dealing With Other Awkward People

So far, I've mostly talked about the other people at parties as outgoing and non awkward extroverts. If you think about it though, there's no way that every single person other than yourself, is a normal, extroverted person, right? Of course, there's no way that that is true. You'll find that you run into plenty of awkward people, like yourself, at parties and gatherings.

Just because two people are awkward, though, this does not guarantee a non awkward interaction. This is not a mathematical equation. Two awkwards do not equal non awkward. As an awkward introvert, you need to know how to deal with other awkward people so that you don't collide into a nuclear explosion of awkwardness. There are two different types of awkward people that you'll need to be aware of.

The Awkward Introvert

When you go to a party, you will often see and/or meet awkward and shy people. You'll be able to identify them fairly quickly. They will be the ones in the corner by themselves or awkwardly scrolling through something on their phone. They should feel comfortable and familiar, because they are you: the awkward introvert.

First thing you need to do is go tell them about this book. In fact, tell everyone you know about this book. The more copies they buy, the better.

Secondly, you need to become their guardian angels. By this point in the book, you should be fairly familiar with the supporting role that your friends can fulfil for you. You should do those things for the awkward introvert. Is it obvious that the awkward introvert is not familiar with everyone's names? Make the introduction! Can you tell the awkward introvert is running low on social energy? Tell them about social havens! (after you finish the book, because Social Havens are covered in the following chapter).

The more you can decrease the AIP (awkwardness inducing potential, for those of you who forgot) in others, the likelihood of you running into awkward situations will decrease. You need to think about this in socio-economic terms. Those who live in areas where the income in higher, tend to have higher incomes as well. You can debate about the actual causality of income trends and all that, but the point is that the less awkward the party is as a whole, the less likely that it will be awkward for you.

The Awkward Extrovert

The awkward extrovert is a dangerous breed. The awkward extrovert is a person who is outgoing and talkative, but they say things that make people feel awkward. For example, an awkward extrovert might join a conversation about everyone's Myers-Brigg personality types and say, "I think people who think Myers-Brigg is accurate are totally dim-witted." Making that comment to a group of people talking about the Myers-Brigg personality is awkward because it offends the whole group. The awkward introvert may think this, but the awkward extrovert will go out of their way to make it known to the group.

The awkward extrovert cannot be helped or saved. Avoid them at all cost. Don't be rude, but don't feel like you need to carry out long conversations with them. You should try to avoid group conversations that the awkward extrovert is a part of as well. The vicariously experienced awkwardness that the awkward extrovert will inevitably attract can be too difficult and embarrassing to witness.

Other awkward people in parties can be dangerous, but not if you know how to deal with them. Familiarize yourself with the differences between the awkward introvert and the awkward extrovert so that you can easily identify them at parties. Now that you know how to handle these two different types of awkward people, you can attend parties without worrying about empathetically feeling other people's awkwardnesses.

Chapter 9 : Finding Social Haven

At every party, there will come a time when you feel drained. Hopefully, this happens at the end of a party, but what about if it happens way too early? I'll go over why leaving too early isn't an option in a later chapter, but there are ways you can find what I'll call "social havens".

I was at a church gathering in college, which was being held at my house. We finished our bible study and the gathering just evolved into a social affair. I was already tired from the socialization during bible study, but I couldn't just leave to go home because it was already at my residence. I was in desperate need of a break from these people.

After a few minutes of staring blankly at a wall while internally screaming, I came up with a plan. I turned on my PlayStation 2 and started Guitar Hero. I pulled out two guitars and asked if anyone wanted to play. One by one, people started gravitating toward the TV to watch people play this game. People started getting so engrossed in the game that most of the conversations stopped. Everyone was too focused on the game. As people attempted increasingly challenging songs, people started cheering and becoming invested in their success. I finally had some time to sit without needing to talk to anyone. It gave me enough rest to push through the rest of the hang out after people lost interest in Guitar Hero.

During a time when I was too socially drained to go on, I created a social haven. A social haven is any thing or situation that lets you stop socializing without being judged. Going outside does not count as a social haven. I know that I suggest going outside a few times as part of escaping awkward situations, but you want to do this sparingly. You don't want to be labeled as the inconsiderate guest who spends all his or her time being absent from the party, do you?

Here are a few examples of social havens that you can create for quick conversational escapes. Wait, hold up. Before I get into this, I must warn against staying on your phone for the entire party. First of all, it's too obvious and lazy. Be a little more creative! The point of the social haven is to get social breaks in a discreet manner. Second, if you sit by yourself with your eyes glued to your phone, people will think that you aren't enjoying the party. We don't want people thinking that you don't like the party. Anyways, here are some examples of some social havens:

The Pet Whisperer

This maneuver requires the host of the party to have a pet. Don't go outside to find a random animal to use though. Although it would be incredibly admirable if you somehow did this, I don't think most people appreciate random wild animals being brought to their party like that. It would be beyond awkward if you were responsible for spreading rabies and other diseases to all the party guests.

Anyhow, the Pet Whisperer social haven is when you spend time away from the people by spending it with the pet. It really doesn't matter what type of pet it is, any pet that is alive will work. A fake backstory like, "I used to have a dog/cat/fish/pony/tiger that looked just like this!" with a solemn look will do the trick. People will assume that you are reliving some happy memories with a deceased pet through this pet. Unless they are clueless and/or heartless, they'll leave you alone.

You can only do this with one pet per social circle, so be wise about which pet you decided to make the subject of your Pet Whisperer. It's best to choose the person who is most likely to hold social gatherings. You can't go around saying every pet you see reminds you of your old pet (unless you live on a farm, I guess). The more non-overlapping social circles you have, though, the more pets you can enroll to be a part in your social haven.

The Long Poop

This one might not be for everyone, especially if you are poop shy. The premise of this social haven is to go to the bathroom and spend up to 30 minutes just sitting on the toilet. The Long Poop requires the least amount of effort out of all the social havens listed here. The Long Poop gives you up to 30 minutes of uninterrupted phone or, possibly, nap time. You can literally do whatever you want while sitting on the toilet. You don't need to make a backstory or act in any way. People tend not to delve too deeply into the details of other peoples bowel movements.

The downside of this social haven is that people will assume that you took a massive dump. Some people will avoid you thinking that you've carried the stench out of the toilet with you, while others might flock to you to show concern, assuming that you are sick or experiencing food poisoning. Neither scenario is desirable, so be careful with the Long Poop.

The Museum Visitor

The Museum Visitor can, usually, only be used once per location of the gathering, and works best at someone's house. The Museum Visitor is when you walk around the house looking at the different photos and objects as if you were in a museum. It helps sell the act if you occasionally mutter comments like, "That's so cute!" or, "I wish I had something like this in my house!" or even, "I wonder where this photo was taken?" Just quietly and slowly walk around observing things. People will leave you alone as long as you look preoccupied.

Don't utilize the Museum Visitor for too long or people might think you are casing the joint to rob it. Also, you can only use this once per location because people expect you to get accustomed to a location once you've visited already. You don't want to find yourself in the situation where you are looking around the place as if it's your first visit and someone asks, "Hey, haven't you been here before?" Awkward.

The DJ

This one is for the music lovers. If you are at a gathering where music is appropriate, volunteer to put on some good music. This will buy you a few minutes as you browse the music collection.

The caveat, though, is that you need to play good music. If the music is not enjoyable for the others, they will remove you from your DJ duties. If you plan on using the DJ social haven, include music research to your arrival planning phase. Look for clues of what type of music the people at the party enjoy. For example, if people have photos at a music festival, look for who headlined at that festival and play their music. If it looks like people attend wine tastings and correcting other's pronunciation of foreign words, put on some douchey classical music.

The Baby Fever

If there are babies at the gathering, you can use them! Babies have the advantage of providing human contact without the troublesome socializing. If someone brings a baby to the gathering, it's totally acceptable to hold the baby and speak gibberish to it. Make it appear that you have baby fever (this works even if you are a guy) and spend time playing with the baby.

There are a few dangers you need to be aware before employing this technique. After I got married, I used this social haven all the time. People around me started having babies left and right, making it fertile ground for this social haven. After around a year, I came to be known as the guy that's "good with babies and kids." This isn't necessarily bad as it can help organically create the Baby Fever social havens in future gatherings, but it does make you the go to guy for baby help.

Recently, I was at a birthday party and I was the first to arrive. Not only was I the first, but mine was the first car parked in a FILO parking situation. I was totally off my arrival planning game that day. The hosts of the party had two babies and I was playing with their daughter when her mother screams and gives me her son to hold. His poop water had leaked through the diaper. She went to go find a change of clothes. For a full 30 seconds I held a toddler with poop water dripping down his leg while desperately trying to avoid touching the poop water.

I was the first attendant and known to enjoy playing with babies. Because I was known to enjoy spending time with babies, the hosts assumed that I would not have a problem helping during this poop leakage crisis. As much as I love the hosts of the party and the baby that dripped poop water out of his diaper, it was truly my worst nightmare.

So in conclusion, social havens can provide much needed social rest, but you can't use it for too long without having unintended consequences. Think of social havens as life lines. Only use them when absolutely necessary.

Chapter 10 : Developing Your Departure Plan

So you've survived the party and now feel that it is appropriate to go back to the sanctuary of your home. Leaving a party sounds straightforward and not worth mentioning, but just like you should develop an arrival plan, you need to prepare a departure plan.

How you arrive at a party will determine the course of the party, but how you leave a party will potentially determine future social interaction with people at the party. So, given the amount of time that impact can have, I would argue that the departure plan is more important than the arrival plan.

Attendance Duration

Before you actually leave the party, you need to think about your attendance duration. Especially if you are the first one to leave, you should think about whether or not you were at the party long enough. If you get in the habit of leaving parties too early, extroverts might assume that you don't like the group. This can lead to misunderstandings and awkward situations. Be sure you feel comfortable about how much time you spent at the party. If you ever hear the phrase, "We never get to hang out because you always leave so early!" then you definitely need to consider extending your party duration.

If at all possible, avoid being the first person to leave the party. Being labelled the person who cannot wait to leave parties isn't good. Sure, the benefit may be that you'll receive less party invitations, but in the long run, you'll be sad and lonely when all your friends hang out without you all the time.

Team Exit

If you are attending a party with a group, then you need to have a consensus to leave before actually leaving the party. To be clear, what I mean by group is the group of people that must leave together by necessity. If you agreed to attend a party with a friend, but drove there separately, this is not what I mean as a group. A group is when people drive in a single car to the party together, and must therefore, leave the party together lest someone be stranded.

Tell me if this sounds familiar. You carpool to a party with a couple friends. You spend a few hours there and have a good time. It's getting late, though, so you look around, trying to rally your carpool mates to leave. You are an awkward introvert, so you don't say this verbally. Instead, you slowly start gathering your things and putting on your jacket. You hope that your friends will take the hint, but they continue their socializing, blissfully ignorant. For the rest of the party, you stand around with your jacket on, pretending that you put it on because you suddenly got cold. This exact situation is why you need a Team Exit.

I feel bad about this, but I usually reject carpooling offers to parties so that I can avoid this situation. I know that I should be more environmentally conscious, but my awkward introvertedness trumps my concern for the environment. I apologize for that. Just know that I am aware of my flaws and am always trying to improve myself.

Fortunately, though, you can feel free to carpool with others as much as you want. You can just set a Team Exit time and agree on it beforehand. If you guys can coordinate this well, you don't need to awkwardly stand around wondering when you are going to get to leave.

Departure Point

As an introvert, I know that the normal protocol in leaving a party is to slip out unnoticed without telling anyone. I know that this is the easiest, but in the long run, this can have harmful effects. When you leave a party without people noticing, you leave yourself vulnerable to a lot of awkward situations. You need to have a clear and distinct Departure Point.

The Departure Point is basically just the time that you leave the party. The point of a Departure

Point isn't for you to document the time you left, but it is for others to know when you stopped being at the party. To minimize future awkward situations, it's important to make sure that everyone knows your Departure Point.

Story time. Let me give you an example of an awkward situation caused by a lack of a Departure Point.

"Hey David! It was great seeing you at the party yesterday!" said Jane Doe.

"Yeah, it was great seeing you too!" I replied.

"Sorry about the mess my ex-boyfriend made," said Jane Doe.

"Uh, what was that?" I asked.

"Near the end of the night. The big, hairy guy who came and trashed the place," answered Jane Doe.

"Oh, yeah. Sure," I said awkwardly without really knowing what she was talking about.

"Yeah. So on that topic though. I'm going to sue him for all the damages and I wanted to see if you could testify in court as a witness," said Jane Doe.

And that is the story of how I committed perjury in a court or law. Just kidding, this didn't really happen to me. Let's just pretend like it did though, so that I can make my point.

What Jane Doe didn't realize was that I left the party before her ex-boyfriend hulked out and damaged her belongings. I was too awkward to correct her and needed to commit to the lie that I saw this incident happen. I could have avoided the entire ordeal if I made my Departure Point very clear and obvious.

The objective of a Departure Point is to make it known to everyone in the party's attendance, precisely the moment you stopped being at the party. People should be able to accurately plot out the time you left on their mental timeline of the party. There are a few methods you can employ to help you define a clear Departure Point.

Some of these methods are as follows:

The Reminder

The Reminder is when you ask several people to remind you when it is a certain time. For example, you can tell people that you need to be home by 9:30 PM, but your phone is out of battery so you don't know the time. You then ask them to remind you when it is 9:15 PM so that you can leave and make it home on time.

If you ask enough people to do this for you, by the time 9:15 PM rolls around, the numerous reminders being thrown at you will cause a big enough splash on the flow of the party that the entire party will know that you left the party at 9:15 PM.

This will make sure people, even the people who you didn't ask the reminder for, will remember that you left the party at 9:15 PM to get home by 9:30 PM.

The False Alarm

Are you or your wife pregnant? Are you expecting news about a job or business deal? Have you heard rumors that your all-time favorite band is planning a guerilla-styled, surprise concert on the rooftops of a nearby city? If yes, then you can use the False Alarm to set your Departure Point.

If you have a situation that warrants you leaving the party to attend to some other matter, then use that to say, "Oh my gosh, that thing happened!" and leave. Include your situation in your small talk topics and try to let as many people know as possible. That way, when you announce that you need to leave because of that situation, people will turn to congratulate you as you leave.

For example, let's say that a family member is pregnant. You can tell people about how excited you are about this member of your family being pregnant. Seed the idea to as many people as you can during your small talk sessions. When you decide you want to leave the party, simply yell out, "She's having the baby!" and leave as you say bye to everyone. Everyone's attention will be on you, allowing you to firmly establish your Departure Point. If anyone asks you later how the baby is, just tell them that it was a false alarm.

The Last Man Standing

The Last Man (or women, of course) Standing will be the least popular for our introverted readers. It is as it sounds, you stay at the party until all the guests have left. It makes me tired just thinking about it.

The only reason I include this as an option, is because it will guarantee that you don't miss anything at the party. No awkward situations about someone mistaking when you left can be had, because you will have left after this person. This method is extremely high cost, high reward.

Chapter 11 : Conclusion

Well there you have it folks, the complete guide to surviving parties for awkward introverts. You now have a full arsenal of tricks and methods to help you go through parties without becoming completely drained or finding yourself in awkward situations. Before you attend your next party, you now know to do the necessary research and preparations to make the party a success.

I don't have much more to say, so I'll keep this short, but I hope that you will be able to use what you learned in this book to go and enjoy the next party, or any type of social gathering, instead of being stressed out the whole time. This book will help you survive parties, but you need to make the conscious decision to go a step further and actually enjoy it. My hope is that the things you learned from this book will help you worry less and be less anxious to give you enough leeway to be able to enjoy the party.

Anyways, thank you so much for reading and I hope that learned some cool things and enjoyed your time! Thanks again!

About the Author

David Shin is a Korean-American consultant with a bachelor's degree in engineering. He enjoys watching movies, playing video games, and day-dreaming about becoming a real life superhero. When he isn't doing something unproductive, David can be found admiring his wife's beauty and thanking God for sending him an angel for a wife.

David really is an awkward introvert who, until this book, was too afraid to follow his dreams of being an author. He honorably obeyed his parents' wishes and obtained an engineering degree and a stable job, but after doing so, he realized it was time to at least make an attempt at being a writer. He really hopes that he'll be able to use phrases like "the best-selling author of..." when he writes the "about the author" on his next book.

Connect with David on:

Facebook :
https://www.facebook.com/AuthorDavidDHShin/
Twitter : @daviddhshin
Instagram : @daviddhshin
Blogger : http://DavidDHShin.blogspot.com

Printed in Great Britain
by Amazon